Simplify
Your Life

Simplify Your Life

By Woodeene Koenig-Bricker

1-special place (discipline to be [get]
together)

Our Sunday Visitor Publishing Division
Our Sunday Visitor, Inc.
Huntington, Indiana 46750

Nihil Obstat: Msgr. Michael Heintz, Ph.D.
Censor Librorum
Imprimatur: ✠ Kevin C. Rhoades
Bishop of Fort Wayne-South Bend
February 22, 2010

Our Sunday Visitor Publishing Division
Our Sunday Visitor, Inc.
200 Noll Plaza
Huntington, IN 46750
1-800-348-2440
bookpermissions@osv.com

ISBN: 978-1-59276-681-9 (Inventory No. T960)
eISBN: 978-1-61278-291-1
LCCN: 2010921392

Cover design by Rebecca J. Heaston
Cover photo: Shutterstock
Interior design by Sherri L. Hoffman

PRINTED IN THE UNITED STATES OF AMERICA

Contents

Introduction

Before we begin, I have a confession to make. I don't live a perfectly simple life. I sometimes wake up in the middle of the night because the worries of the day won't let me sleep. I get migraines because I can't accomplish everything I think I should in the time I have to do it. I've been known to circle around my "to-do" lists like a bloodhound that has lost the scent of the trail.

So why am I writing this book?

Because my life is significantly simpler than it was just a few years ago. No, I didn't divest myself of all my possessions, leave family and friends behind, and become a hermit. I still live in the same house, do the same kind of work, and have the same friends. While I'd never claim to have all the answers as to how to create an ideally simple life, I can honestly say that I now live a life that generally reflects not just my external activities, but my internal convictions as well.

I wish I could say that the changes I've made were the result of some deep spiritual insight, but they weren't. In fact, they weren't exactly my idea at all. For most of my life, I took pride in my crowded calendar, my multiple responsibilities, my ability to do two or three things at once. Then, one day, I was diagnosed with a chronic illness that forced me to cut back on many of my activities. I couldn't continue to do things the way I had anymore. I had no choice. I had to simplify my life.

When I first had to change the way I lived, I did what I always do when faced with any challenge: I researched it. I checked out armloads of books from the library and placed numerous orders on Amazon for every book I could find on "Simple Living."

What I got out of all my reading was the idea that if I were just better organized, my life would be simpler. Because I am somewhat organizationally challenged, that made sense. Organize my way to the simple life! I'm on it!

I bought matching baskets for everything. I decided I would have only two sets of towels per person — one to use, one to wash. (Hey, if it worked for Mother Teresa and her saris, it might work for my bathrooms!) I made lists for the pantry and freezer so I would always know what food was available. I stopped matching my socks, simply tossing them in a drawer and pulling out a pair when needed as some simplicity guru suggested. I compiled notebooks and color-coded lists. In short, I worked very hard at making things simpler.

Needless to say, it wasn't quite the success I'd hoped. In fact, it made things more complicated. Now I had to update the food lists each time I went shopping. If I didn't do laundry every day, I had the choice of using a wet towel or drip-drying. The unmatched socks idea worked okay, but I soon got tired of pawing through piles to find what I was looking for. I was getting more crossed off my "to-do" list because I was more organized, but many of the things I was getting done revolved around staying organized.

Even though I had the appearance of a simpler life, it really wasn't all that simple, because I hadn't made the internal, spiritual changes that are necessary for real, lasting, meaningful change. I had merely rearranged the deck chairs on my own personal *Titanic.* That's when I realized that if I didn't want to end up drowning, I had to go down in the hold and rebuild the hull of my existence.

That's the real reason I'm writing this book.

I want to share with you some of the ways I've changed my life so that I'm more at peace, more bal-anced, and more centered than at any other point in my adult life. My life is simpler than it was, absolutely; but more important, my life is now much richer and more fulfilling. And ultimately, isn't that what we all want? A life in which we can have the time to appreciate what we have, enjoy our friends and family, create, celebrate, and "be," instead of always having to "do." A life that is focused on activities that nurture the soul and enrich the spirit instead of destroying them. The life that Jesus promised when he said that he came so that we "may have life, and have it abundantly."

CHAPTER 1

The Simple Life

KISS: Keep It Simple, Sweetheart

Life is like art. You have to work hard to keep it simple and still have meaning.

— CHARLES DE LINT

What complicates your life the most?

What's keeping you from having a simpler life?

If you were to ask a dozen people, you'd probably get a dozen different answers, ranging from work to finances to relationships. However, when we think about what complicates and stresses our lives, those things generally fall into one of four categories: things, people, activities, and mind/body/spirit.

We'll take a look at each of these areas in turn, but before we do, let's talk a little bit about what makes up a simple life. Do any of these resonate with you?

> The ordinary arts we practice every day at home.
>
> — St. Thomas More

> To find the universal elements enough; to find the air and the water exhilarating; to be refreshed by a morning walk or an evening saunter... to be thrilled by the stars at night; to be elated over a bird's nest or a wildflower in spring.
>
> — John Burroughs

> Breath in your nostrils, light in your eyes, flowers at your feet, duties at your hand, the path of right just before you... life's plain, common work as it comes.
>
> — Robert Lewis Stevenson

Basic Joys

Like the saint and the poet, I think most of us would agree that the simple life consists of being aware and appreciative of the basic joys of daily existence. Deep down, we know that drinking a fresh cup of coffee as we watch the sunrise brings deeper satisfaction than buying the latest electronic device, but we still get caught up in the consumerism and "do-erism" that pervades our culture.

If we really want to change, if we really want a simpler life, we have to stop and take a long, hard look at our lives. We have to figure out what it is that we want. Only then we can figure out how to get there.

> *Simplicity is making the journey of this life with just baggage enough.*
> — CHARLES DUDLEY WARNER

The first step in creating a simpler life is to envision what a simple life would look like for you. What constitutes a simple life for you will not be the same as it is for me. A simple life has a different meaning and different elements for each person, depending on your personality, your state of life, your talents, and your responsibilities. For me, a simple life means having the time to do what's most important to me, creating a space that is filled with only the things that bring me joy, getting rid of ideas that aren't in alignment with my spiritual values, and finding ways to bring beauty into my daily existence. I don't really care where I live, for instance. But you might. Your definition of the simple life may include living in the country, so that you can be close to nature. I don't like to cook, so a simple life for me includes access to takeout. However, your simple life might allow time each evening to prepare a home-cooked meal.

The point is that only you can define your own simple life. It's not a one-size-fits-all pattern. Your simple life is just that — yours!

> *If you want a golden rule that will fit everybody, this is it. Have nothing in your house that you do not know to be useful, or believe to be beautiful.*
>
> — WILLIAM NORRIS

One Perfect Day

What would you like to experience in a "perfect" day? What time would you get up? What would you do first? What activities would you absolutely want included? Who is with you? What are you wearing? What do you eat? What does your environment look like? Write out all the details you can think of, including the color of the walls in your ideal home, the type of furniture, the car you drive. Try to make it as vivid and as real as you can. Really try to *live* your ideal simple day.

Don't get caught up in trying to figure out what's possible in your current life. Free your imagination. Allow the Holy Spirit to guide you in envisioning what your ideal life might look like. Censor that little voice that pipes up to tell you, "That'll never happen!" Remember, every change begins with a thought, a dream. If you want to simplify your life, first you have to imagine and believe that you can simplify it.

Next, pray over your ideal life. God, who is the author of your imagination, knows what it is you want, because he created you. He put those dreams into your mind and heart. So ask him to give you the wisdom and courage to make the necessary changes.

Finally, remember that the longest journey begins with the first step. Congratulations! You've just taken that first step on your path to a simpler life!

Take Away

You have to first believe that change is possible if you want to simplify your life.

CHAPTER 2

Objects Lesson

One Thing, Two Thing, Red Thing, Blue Thing

He who knows that enough is enough will always have enough.

— Lao Tzu

One of the major barriers to a simpler life is *things*. Look around the room you're in right now. I'd be willing to bet that you have more "stuff" in your life than you really need.

Don't be embarrassed. Almost all of us have more than we need. If we want to have a simpler life, however, we have to get rid of some of the objects that fill our lives. There are several practical and psychological reasons for this.

First, taking care of objects eats up time and energy. The more things, the more time and energy. Every time you bring an item into your house, you are trading some portion of your life to take care of it. This is true even for "time-saving" devices. A dishwasher saves time and water, but you still have to keep it clean and serviced. Using a vacuum cleaner is easier than taking up the carpets and beating them, but you must empty the bag. The invisible price tag on every item is its lifetime cost in care.

> *The cost of a thing is the amount of… life which is required to be exchanged for it, immediately or in the long run.*
>
> — HENRY DAVID THOREAU

Second, more stuff means more clutter. I fell into the trap of thinking that the way to manage my possessions was to organize them. However, organized clutter is still clutter. A cute basket in which to put your junk mail doesn't eliminate the junk mail. Clutter drains your energy, sucks up your time, and generally adds to your stress — and stress certainly contributes to a less than simple life.

Third, stuff breeds stuff. Not literally, of course, although I'm not quite sure about clothes hangers. It's just that almost nothing comes by itself. You get a new TV, for instance, and you end up with a remote, cables that you may or may not need, packaging, instructions, a warranty, and assorted other things that you have to do something with, even if you just throw them out.

Finally, having too many objects keeps our eyes fixed on the material instead of the spiritual, to our ultimate peril. Remember the parable of the rich man in Luke 12:16-21:

> [16]The land of a rich man produced abundantly. [17]And he thought to himself, "What should I do, for I have no place to store my crops?" [18]Then he said, "I will do this: I will pull down my barns and build larger ones, and there I will store all my grain and my goods. [19]And I will say to my soul, Soul, you have ample goods laid up for many years; relax, eat, drink, be merry." [20]But God said to him, "You fool! This very night your life is being demanded of you. And the things you have prepared, whose will they be?" [21]So it is with those who store up treasures for themselves but are not rich towards God.

"Just Right!"

Now, before you think I'm going to suggest that you give up all your worldly goods and join a monastery, I'm not.

I've had the honor of going behind the walls of a Carmelite cloister, where the nuns live in deliberate poverty, and even they had "stuff." Less than I have for sure, but they still had things that weren't absolutely necessary for mere existence. If they, whose lives are dedicated to simplicity, can have a few things because they are beautiful, or fun, or "just because," so can we.

Then she lay down in the third bed and it was just right.
— *GOLDILOCKS AND THE THREE BEARS*

The idea is to be like Goldilocks and find what's right for you. Not too much, not too little, but just enough. Keep in mind that what constitutes "just enough" for me won't be the same as for you. The First Lady needs a much more extensive and formal wardrobe than a stay-at-home mom. That's not good or bad; it's just a fact. Don't be tempted to compare your "just right" with that of anyone else, but figure it out for yourself.

How do you determine what's "just right" when it comes to your stuff?

One rule is that if you haven't used it in a year, get rid of it. That works for a lot of people, but it's never worked for me. I have objects that I've never used and probably never will use — my grandmother's treadle sewing machine — but I want to keep them. What's more useful for me is to ask: Do I love this? Does this make me smile? Would I regret it if I lost it? Most of the time, an honest answer will tell me what I need to do with the object — keep it or let someone else have it.

However (insert sound of other shoe dropping), I have a slight little tendency to hoard objects. Unlike some of my friends, I don't get a rush of joy when I take a load to the St. Vincent de Paul store. Ever since I gave away my blender and then realized I actually did use it at the holidays, I've been plagued with "what if." What if I need this? What if I miss it? What if I want it back? If you are like me in this regard, you may need to take a strong stand with yourself and apply the "Decimation Rule."

We tend to think that "decimation" means total destruction, but it doesn't. It means "removal of a tenth" and refers to a Roman military discipline for mutinous or cowardly soldiers. Instead of punishing everyone, a unit would be divided into groups of 10. Each group drew lots, and the unfortunate soldier in each group would be executed by his comrades, usually by stoning or clubbing. One tenth of each group was thereby eliminated.

This technique works well for smaller items that tend to accumulate, such as books, vases, coffee mugs, and T-shirts. I apply it one of two ways. If I'm feeling particularly bold, I simply start counting and remove every tenth item. If I'm not up to that sort of random selection, I first count all the objects that I'm dealing with. Let's say I have 25 books stacked next to my bed. (Yes, I've been known to have that many.) I need to get rid of 2.5 of them; so, depending on how I'm feeling, I choose either two or three books and discard them.

Decimation isn't as hard as it sounds; in fact, it can be quite satisfying because it is self-limiting. You know exactly how many things you need to deal with, and after you've made the decision, you don't have to think about the rest of them. At least not for today.

Another way to simplify the number of objects in your life is to make a rule that you will never bring something into the house without first getting rid of a like object. If you get a new pair of shoes, then an old pair has to be removed. Again, this works well for some people, but if it creates more stress, don't do it. A way that works better for me is to put off all purchases over $25 (except for food and medication) for twenty-four hours. If I still want or need the item, then I'll buy it. About half the time I realize that I was caught up in the thrill of a bargain, and I don't really need or even want what I was going to buy.

One Step at a Time

Cutting down on the amount of stuff in your life can feel overwhelming, and the temptation is to quit before you begin. But remember, you don't have to do it all right this minute. Pick one room or a corner of a room or a drawer and start there. Spend ten minutes today, ten minutes tomorrow, ten minutes the next day. If you eliminate a little bit each day, you'll soon discover that the overwhelming mountain of stuff has become a manageable molehill of objects that you actually use, enjoy, and appreciate.

Take Away

If you want to make immediate progress in simplifying your life, cut down on clutter.

CHAPTER 3

Relationships

What's Love Got to Do with It?

Man is a knot, a web, a mesh into which relationships are tied.

— ANTOINE DE SAINT-EXUPÉRY,
FLIGHT TO ARRAS

Relationships are one of the things that complicate our lives in a big way. Jimmy Buffett puts it like this in *Fruitcakes*: "Now here comes the big one. Relationships! We all got 'em. We all want 'em. What do we do with 'em?"

What *do* we do with our relationships? How can we make them simpler?

It's not easy, because unlike objects, we can't just get rid of people. We can't line up everyone in our life, have them count off and discard every tenth one, tempting as that might be.

Dealing with relationships differs between those who are with us for life because of blood or marriage and those with whom we choose to associate, which includes our friends, neighbors, and even work colleagues.

Family Matters

Let's look at family first — those people we can't get rid of, no matter what. Fortunately, we don't usually want to be rid of these people (although there can be exceptions). Often, the problems that complicate these relationships come about because we don't spend enough time with those we love. Rarely is it because we spend too much time together. (Spouses of the newly retired may be the exception to the rule.)

The solution here is a two-step process. First, we need to eliminate some of the things and relationships that drain our time and energy. Then, we need to invest time and energy in being with these people who are permanently sewn into the fabric of our lives. We need to be fully and completely present to these people when we are with them. It doesn't matter if it is your spouse, your children, your parents, or other family members. When you make time to talk with them, share experiences, make memories, and merely be together, your relationships with those you care about most deeply are bound to improve.

> *Piglet sidled up to Pooh from behind. "Pooh!" he whispered.*
>
> *"Yes, Piglet?"*
>
> *"Nothing," said Piglet, taking Pooh's paw. "I just wanted to be sure of you."*
>
> — A.A. MILNE

Is This What I Want?

Then there are those other relationships. It might seem odd to say that if you wish to simplify your relationships you have to analyze and prioritize them, but that's the fact of the matter.

There are a lot of ways to think about this, but one that has worked for me is to make a list of all the people I interact with during a week (excluding family members). Include people you work with, people you see casually, close friends, even online friends.

Next, take a deep breath and divide them into four categories.

1. People you have to be with (such as coworkers).
2. People you want to be with.
3. People you feel obligated to be with.
4. People you merely encounter but aren't involved with.

The trickiest division will be people you have to be with and people you feel obligated to be with, but think of it this way. If you *have* to be with someone, it's because you will encounter them with no effort on your part (the guy in the next cubicle at work). If you have a choice about seeing a person *and* if you feel guilty when you don't, then he or she is an obligation. Trust your intuition as you place people in their categories. Be honest. Don't pretend that you want to be with Cousin Eloise when, deep down, you know she and her ten cats are an obligation. No one will see this list except you. If you must, put it through a shredder when you're done.

Once you've made your lists, determine how much time you spend with the people in each category. Not how much time you *want* to spend, but how much time you *actually* spend. You can put down minutes or percentage or just "a lot," "too much," "not enough." Remember this is just for you, so it doesn't matter how you calculate it.

Undoubtedly you'll spend the most time with people you have to be with. If you are spending *all* of your time with those people, however, while those on your "want to see" list languish, you might want to take a look at how you are divvying up your life.

This is one area in which you must be brutally honest with yourself. If you say you want to be with someone, but you aren't spending any time together, it's for one of two reasons: Either you actually don't want to spend time with them or you need to exercise the discipline to get together. To quote Yoda from *Star Wars*, "Do or do not. There is no 'try.'"

The time you spend with people whom you encounter but aren't closely involved with is usually structured and self-limited, so there's not much you can do about it. It's not that these people aren't important; it's just there isn't any reason to spend more time than necessary with them. What might surprise you are the people who fall into this category. Your doctor could be one. You see him regularly, but he isn't someone you would hang out with. So might the grocery store clerk.

Then there are those people you feel obliged to be with. This is the one area in which you can actually make some changes that will simplify your life, depending on why you feel obligated to be with them. If your obligation stems from duty — such as visiting your great-aunt in the nursing home because you are her only living relative — then the best you can do is decide how much time and energy you want to devote to her and then live with that decision.

If, however, you feel obligated to spend time with someone because you've committed to doing something you really don't want to do, or because of a past relationship, it may be time to end or at least reduce the amount of time you spend together.

This is tough; no question about it. It may require that you say "no" to someone when it would be much easier to go with the flow. It could mean that you have to face the fact that someone who once was a close friend isn't any more; that your lives have gone in different directions and you no longer have the interests or activities in common that once kept you together. It will almost certainly require you to make some choices you won't want to make.

> *To know when to go away and when to come closer is the key to any lasting relationship.*
>
> — DOMÉNICO CIERI ESTRADA

It's Your Decision

The question you have to ask yourself is this: Is the pain of changing the time and energy you spend on certain relationships worth the payoff in simplifying your life? I can't answer that for you. No one can but you. If you decide that visiting Cousin Eloise and her ten cats every week is an obligation, but you would rather do that than hurt her feelings, so be it. If you choose to socialize with your coworkers instead of having dinner with the person you say is your best friend, so be it. If you elect to chat online rather than visit your next-door neighbor, so be it. Just remember: When you consciously make the choice, it's easier to live with the consequences. And that alone can make relationship issues much simpler.

The challenge here is that relationships aren't like things. You do have to consider the other people involved as well as your moral responsibilities. Sometimes, God puts people into our lives for a reason, and even if we find it inconvenient or difficult, deep down we know that the relationship is serving a greater purpose: maybe to help us develop patience or compassion, or to give that person something that only we can provide. That's why deciding which relationships to keep and which to change requires prayer. Before we take any action that would irreparably alter a relationship, we need to ask the Holy Spirit for wisdom and guidance. If God is telling you to remain where you are, you need to pay attention. Likewise, if you get the sense that it's time to move on, you need to obey.

Of all the areas in our lives, dealing with relationships is the one where we can be assured that God will give us the direction we need exactly when we need it. He is, after all, in the business of creating eternal relationships.

Take Away

You have to work at building relationships. You also need to work at simplifying them.

CHAPTER 4

"More Stuff"

The Daze of Our Lives

Our life is frittered away by detail. Simplify, simplify, simplify! I say, let your affairs be as two or three, and not a hundred or a thousand; instead of a million count half a dozen, and keep your accounts on your thumbnail.
— HENRY DAVID THOREAU

The next major area that complicates life is a bit like good art: It's hard to describe, but you know it when you see it. It has to do with your physical environment, your big-ticket items such as your house, and the structure of your day. Unlike ordinary stuff, "more stuff" is composed of those complicating factors that are so big, you don't consciously think about them on a regular basis. They simply form the backdrop of your life. This makes them virtual black holes, sucking up enormous amounts of physical space, energy, and time.

I divide them into four broad categories that make sense to me: Hearth and Home, Media/Entertainment, Routine Maintenance, and Commitments. If these categories don't appeal to you, feel free to make your own divisions. And if one of these areas isn't a problem for you, go right ahead and skip over it. After all, we do want to make the process of simplification as simple as possible!

Hearth and Home

I'm sure you've heard the saying, "Don't sweat the small stuff." Although that statement is true, it's equally true that if we want to simplify our lives, we will need to sweat the big stuff, at least some of the time.

Get rid of unused large appliances, furniture, and fixtures.

Unless you have a very good reason for keeping big-ticket items you aren't using, don't hang on to them for the proverbial "just in case." I have a friend who has stored a toilet in her garage for years, just in case the one in her bathroom breaks. It's taken up space and been an inconvenience and an eyesore. For *years*. It's not like toilets are a rare commodity. If she needed one, she could find one relatively inexpensively. And it wouldn't have years' worth of spider webs in it.

Empty your storage units and vow never to rent another one.

Storage units are a sure sign you have way too much stuff. The only reason to rent one is for a temporary (i.e., a month or less) staging site. I rented one when I had to suddenly move my mother out of her home into assisted living, but it was just until I could sort out what she wanted to keep and what would be going to St. Vincent's.

Reconsider your desire for "toys."

Do you really need to own a boat, a jet ski, an airplane, a motor home, skis, or specialized sports equipment? If you only use such items a few times a year, you can rent them when you want them. That's a whole lot simpler than having to maintain and store something you rarely use.

Evaluate your need for a vacation home or timeshare.

Like an expensive toy, a vacation home or timeshare you use only one or two times a year may cost you more than you think. Unless you absolutely love the location, would you be happier spending the same amount of money seeing other parts of the world on holiday? An honest answer will tell you what you should be doing.

> *Better is a handful of quietness than two hands full of toil and a striving after the wind.*
> — ECCLESIASTES 4:6

Think about downsizing.

Moving into a smaller home isn't just for retirees. If you purge your house of unneeded stuff, you may find you don't need as much room. A smaller house can be cheaper, easier to maintain, and generally simpler to live in. This is one of those areas in which only you can decide what's right for you and what will make you comfortable. If you have a big family or if you live in your dream house, ignore this idea.

Downsizing your car may be another option for simplification, especially if you are still driving a huge SUV or "gas hog." It's not necessary to go so small that you and your family are like a dozen clowns stuffed in a miniature vehicle, but you may not need an oversized van, either. A smaller car is easier to drive and park as well as cheaper to fuel — all of which can make your life simpler.

If you are feeling very radical, you might consider getting rid of your car altogether. Although eliminating auto ownership isn't an option for many of us, owning and operating a car is a major expense and often a major headache. If public transportation is a viable alternative, or if you live close enough to shopping and work to walk or bike, you might think about going car-less. But as you consider this, be sure to factor in things like the extra time it may take to go places and your personal level of frustration. Getting rid of your car and then bumming rides might make your life a little simpler, but it's not fair to your friends and family.

Streamline tasks at home.

We live in a do-it-yourself society. As a matter of pride, we think we should take care of everything in our homes by ourselves. Consider, though, that there are people who make their living doing the things you either dislike or don't do well. While it's always a balancing act between spending the extra money to hire someone and the payoff in terms of simplifying your life, it's something to think about.

I don't like yard work. As a matter of fact, I really hate yard work. I can mow my own lawn, and I have mowed my own lawn, but I'd rather cut back somewhere else and have someone mow it for me. It's a win/win. Somebody gets the work; I get out of mowing the lawn.

Another idea is to delegate tasks to other family members. If you try to do everything yourself, you're bound to feel overwhelmed. Remember the old saying: Many hands make light work!

Everything should be made as simple as possible, but not one bit simpler.

— ALBERT EINSTEIN

A Place for Everything

Ever spend way too much time looking for something you know you have, only to end up buying a replacement because you didn't put it back the last time you used it? "A place for everything and everything in its place" is one of the cardinal rules of simplification. If you can't figure out where to put something, maybe you really don't need it after all!

Media/Entertainment

Another complicating factor of modern life is the flood of media. A study from the University of California, San Diego, says that Americans now spend three out of every four waking hours being inundated by information. The report says that the average American consumes 34 gigabytes and 100,000 words over the course of about 12 hours every day. Nearly half of that time is spent watching television; about a quarter on the computer; and the rest on radio, print media, telephones, computer games, recorded music, movies, and other sources.[1]

One of the ways we can simplify our lives is to cut back on the amount of time and energy we hand over to technology.

Go on a "Media Diet"

Reduce the time you spend watching TV, on the Internet, listening to the radio, and receiving information in other ways. You don't have to be plugged in 24/7

---

1. "Data Overload: Americans in the Digital Age" — *Sphere News.* www.sphere.com/tech/article/uc-san-diego-researchers-attempt-to-quantify-digital-revolution/19282576.

to know what's going on in the world. Trust me. If it's important enough, you'll learn about it soon enough. In the meantime, knowing about every disaster in every corner of the world as it's happening creates a constant state of fear and apprehension. If you must get a regular news/media fix, watch one newscast, read one paper, check a few Web sites — but do it only once a day.

Cut Back on Communication

Once upon a time, people actually had to be in their homes or businesses to receive a phone call. They didn't have a phone with them all the time. This "antiquated" era was fewer than 20 years ago! Nowadays, we not only have cell phones, we have e-mail, IM, Skype, Twitter, Facebook, podcasts, streaming video, and undoubtedly something new created between the time I write this and the time you read it. You could spend your entire life "communicating" without ever actually talking to anyone.

To simplify this, you'll need to exercise discipline. Only check your e-mail at designated times. Limit your phone use (both cell and landline). Don't use instant-message services to relieve boredom. Control the technology; don't let it control you.

Admission time: I'm a communication technology junkie. This isn't one of the areas that causes me stress. If it doesn't stress you, either, forget I mentioned it!

Routine Maintenance

Routines are one of the easier and most effective ways to simplify your life. While a thoughtless routine can become a rut, many routines are actually beneficial.

Think how much time and effort it would take if you had to figure out how to brush your teeth every morning! A good routine is basically a streamlined system for accomplishing regular, repetitive tasks. It allows our mind to go on autopilot for a few minutes while we continue to function efficiently.

> *The ability to simplify means to eliminate the unnecessary so that the necessary may speak.*
>
> — HANS HOFMANN

Most people benefit from established routines in some of the following areas, but every family is little different. Adopt only those routines that fit your lifestyle and make your life simpler rather than add one more thing to the "to-do" list.

- Find a way to deal with mail and paperwork by creating a mail center and a process for handling bills as soon as they come in.
- Develop a plan for cleaning the house. You'll find dozens of books and Web sites devoted to simplifying housework. Find one that works for you.
- Keep your work area clean. It doesn't matter if it's a desk or a kitchen counter; make sure it's clear each evening, ready for the next day's activities.
- Figure out your filing. A simple alphabetical filing system in a file box or cabinet works for most people; but again, you'll find entire books and Web sites dedicated to developing a system that is right for your needs.

- Set up a calendar for recurring activities such as car servicing, teeth cleaning, and smoke detector battery changing.
- Have a plan for morning and evening. Every parent knows the benefits of having a routine at bedtime for young children, but even adults benefit from a regular schedule with planned activities. You don't have to be a slave to the routine, but having a plan will make your overall life much easier and less complicated.
- Schedule "down time." Giving yourself some space in your day allows you to handle the unexpected much more easily and without getting frazzled.

Commitments

Ever have the feeling that if you had one more commitment in your life, you'd need to *be* committed? Too much to do and too little time to do it is a major complaint for most people.

The solution is straightforward, but you probably won't like it.

Say "no" more often.

We don't like to say "no" to people because we are afraid they won't like us or they will think poorly of us. So we say "yes" to things we don't want to do and assume responsibilities we end up resenting.

If you truly want to simplify your life, wait at least 24 hours before giving an answer about taking on anything new. Very few things require an immediate response. Say instead, "I've got to think about this before

I commit to it. I'll let you know tomorrow." Then listen to your instincts. Does this excite you? Do you have time to do it? Is it something that someone else could do just as well? Honest answers will tell you what's best for you and your family.

One subtly deceptive way we can become overcommitted without realizing it is through doing "good works." If you are spending more time than you should at your church (be honest with yourself and you'll know if you are), or if your family is becoming resentful of the time you spend doing volunteer work, the only answer is to cut back. Let someone else have the chance to help. It isn't all your responsibility.

It's okay to be selective in what you bring into your life. In fact, if you want a simpler life, it's absolutely essential.

Take Away

Simplifying your life requires looking at all aspects and being willing to make difficult decisions in order to implement lasting change.

CHAPTER 5

Body/Mind/Spirit

You Can't Have One without the Other

A sound mind in a sound body is a short but full description of a happy state in this world.

— JOHN LOCKE

I have learned (and still am learning) that it's great to have an efficient way to simplify paperwork; but in the long run, it's more important to simplify from the inside out.

So now we get to the hard part. The place where change is more difficult, but infinitely more rewarding: the body/mind/spirit.

Let's Get Physical

What does improving your physical health have to do with simplifying your life? Although feeling better might not make life simpler, being unhealthy definitely will complicate it. Doctor visits, prescriptions, hospitalization, surgery, physical therapy, tests, restricted activities . . . the time, expense, and general frustration is incalculable. So getting healthy and staying that way is a simplification that will pay off for your entire life.

I'm sure you know the drill — we all do. Eat better. Exercise. Lose weight if necessary. We (and I include myself in this) just have to make the decision to do it and then ask for the strength to follow through.

One area I would like to talk a little about, though, is relieving stress. Stress is a major complicating factor for most of our lives. Google it and you'll come up with more than 35 million sites! According to *Healthy People 2000*, a report from the U.S. Department of Health and Human Services:

- Between 70 and 80 percent of all visits to the doctor are for stress-related and stress-induced illnesses.

- Stress contributes to 50 percent of all illness in the United States.
- The cost of job stress is estimated at $200 billion annually.

Stress is killing us, literally. Little wonder that we have a desire to eliminate as much as possible from our lives. Unfortunately, stress seems to be a natural part of the human condition. Cortisol, the hormone created as a response to real or perceived threats (stress), can be traced and measured in bodily remains, particularly hair. Research shows that ancient Nubians, Egyptians, and Peruvians produced high amounts of cortisol, higher than most people have today. Of course, the stressors aren't the same, but our bodies don't distinguish between running from a hungry crocodile and dealing with the IRS.

The bad news is that stress is a fact of human life. Jesus tells us in Matthew 6:34, "Do not be anxious about tomorrow, for tomorrow will be anxious for itself. Let the day's own trouble be sufficient for the day." Sounds to me like he is saying we will have stressors in life as long as we are on earth.

The good news is that though it might be a fact of life, it doesn't have to be the controlling factor of life. In the end, stress isn't something that happens to us, but something that we do to ourselves.

Don't believe me? Consider this scenario: You're under a deadline. The minutes are ticking by. You look at how much you have left to do, and you start to panic. Then, all of a sudden, you realize you've been looking at

Here are a few proven ways to de-stress.

Get a massage.	Take a nap.
Take a warm bath.	Pray the Rosary.
Listen to relaxing music.	Meditate.
Have a cup of tea.	Pet an animal.
Keep a journal.	Play with a child.
Drink more water.	Do something creative.
Take a walk.	Allow yourself to play.
Read a good book.	Do nothing. Just *be*.
Get outdoors, especially in the sunlight.	

the wrong clock — you actually have another hour. I'm willing to bet your stress level just dropped measurably. Are you any further along in your task? No. Do you have any more time than you had a few minutes ago? No. All that changed is how you feel.

That's how we simplify stress. By learning to decompress and change the ways we feel.

> *There must be quite a few things that a hot bath won't cure, but I don't know many of them.*
>
> —SYLVIA PLATH

It's All in Your Mind

Did you know that the average person has about 70,000 thoughts a day? Learning how to control our thoughts will simplify our lives. In fact, Scripture tells us to do just that: "Take every thought captive" (2 Cor 10:5).

How do we capture those elusive thoughts that race through our minds?

One of the best ways is to be present in the moment. The past is gone; the future isn't yet here. All we've got is the here and now. By doing one thing at a time, being aware of what you are doing, and putting your full attention on each activity, you can eliminate some of the chatter in your head. If you're washing dishes, don't think about mowing the lawn. Just think about the water, the soap, the plate in your hand. If you're mowing the lawn, be aware of the smell of the freshly cut grass, the sound of the motor, the color of the field. As novelist Storm Jameson says, "The only way to live is to accept each minute as an unrepeatable miracle, which is exactly what it is: a miracle and unrepeatable."

> *God speaks to all individuals through what happens to them moment by moment.*
>
> — J.P. DeCaussade

Spiritus Tuus

It might seem heretical to think about your faith as one of the things that complicates your life. After all, our religion is supposed to be the foundation of our existence. It's supposed to bring us comfort and sustenance.

All of that is true. You can't have a truly simple life without a deep spiritual underpinning. Faith and practice, however, can be two different things. The reality is that spiritual faith can bring untold comfort, but spiritual practice can add stress and complications.

Let me explain.

Do you think you have to do certain things to be a good Catholic? I'm not talking about obligations such as attending Mass on Sunday. I'm talking about optional devotions such as praying the Rosary, saying the Divine Office, or attending daily Mass.

While all of these are good things, not all good things are right for everyone. I've always taken comfort in the fact that St. Thérèse of Lisieux said, "It's a terrible thing to admit, but saying the Rosary takes it out of me more than any hair shirt... Try as I will, I cannot meditate on the mysteries of the Rosary. I just cannot fix my mind on them."

If you want to simplify your spiritual practices, find one thing that resonates in your heart and soul and focus on it. For me, it's sitting quietly in silent prayer before I begin my day. For you, it might be reading Scripture. (Or even praying the Rosary!) It doesn't really matter what it is, as long as you choose it consciously. Don't let your life be ruled by someone else's idea of what you should be doing. And always remember: "For everything there is a season, and a time for every matter under heaven" (Eccles 3:1). What's right for you now might not be right in the future. You may decide to do something different next year, or even next week.

And that's okay, too.

Take Away

Simplifying your life requires changing the way you think, as well as the way you act, because the body and mind work together.

CHAPTER 6

The Environment

We're All on This Planet Together

Where my caravan has rested, flowers I leave you on the grass.

— MONICA DICKENS

Simply Good Stewardship

It might seem a little odd to talk about the environment in a book on simplifying our lives, but over the course of his papacy, Pope Benedict XVI has stressed time and again that we are all on this planet together. It is part of our moral obligation to care for the earth and its inhabitants, both plant and animal.

As he puts it:

> We must... demonstrate with our example, with our own style of life, that we are speaking of a message in which we ourselves believe, one by which it's possible to live. We want to ask the Lord to help us all live the faith, the responsibility of the faith, in such a way that our style of life becomes a form of witness, and that our words express the faith in a credible way as an orientation in our time.[1]

Live simply that others may simply live.
— MOHANDAS GANDHI

Going Easy on the Earth

Fortunately, many things that have positive environmental effects also make your life easier! It's true. Once again, it's a matter of making efforts to cut out waste and use your resources wisely... and simply.

---

1. August 6, 2008.

Need more specifics? These suggestions from *100 Ways to Save the Environment* will help get you started.

- Keep your thermostat at 68 in winter and 78 in summer.
- Lower the thermostat on your water heater to 120.
- Turn off lights when leaving a room.
- Wash clothes with warm or cold water instead of hot.
- Use compact fluorescent light bulbs to save money and energy.
- Plant trees to shade your home and outdoor air-conditioning units.
- Avoid using leaf blowers and other dust-producing equipment.
- Leave grass clippings on the yard; they decompose and return nutrients to the soil.
- Minimize pesticide use.
- Consider installing a sprinkler system to maximize watering efficiency.
- Use recycled paper and use both sides of old paper for notes, scratch paper, etc.
- Use ceramic coffee mugs instead of disposable cups.
- Ignite charcoal barbecues with a charcoal chimney instead of lighter fluid.
- Check and fix any water leaks.
- Wash and dry only full loads of laundry and dishes.
- Buy items in bulk, from loose bins when possible, to avoid wasteful packaging.

- Maintain and repair durable products instead of buying new ones.
- Reuse items like bags and containers when possible.
- Shop with a canvas bag instead of using paper and plastic bags.
- Buy rechargeable batteries for frequently-used devices.[2]

Taking Care

It can be overwhelming to wonder what we can possibly do to affect larger, more complex environmental concerns. But the good news is that by taking individual responsibility for reusing, recycling, and conservation, we can rest assured that at least we are making "our little corner of the world" better... and in the process, preserving what we have been given for future generations as well.

Take Away

A simple life benefits both you and the environment.

---

2. List originated by Sustainable Environment for Quality of Life, Centralina Council of Governments. www.4CCOG.org.

CHAPTER 7

Simply Abundant

Growing in Gratitude

Gratitude is the memory of the heart.

— FRENCH PROVERB

By now, you probably have some idea of what it will take to create a simpler life. There's just one more thing I want to share with you. Once I figured it out and began doing it regularly, I can honestly say that it literally changed everything. It's the key that unlocked a simpler life.

What is this "magic" solution?

Grow in gratitude.

I can almost hear your sigh of frustration. "Gratitude? That's it?"

Yes, living in a constant state of gratitude is probably most important thing you can do if you truly desire to simplify and enrich your life. But gratitude may not be what you think.

Not What You Think

We've generally been taught that gratitude is one of two things: It's the act of saying "thank you" when we receive a gift or a favor, or it's a feeling of thankfulness. I can remember reading 1 Thessalonians 5:18 ("Give thanks in all circumstances; for this is the will of God in Christ Jesus for you") during a particularly difficult time in my life and thinking, "I'm just supposed to suck up my feelings and tell God how happy I am that all of this is happening to me? Not going to happen."

I was misreading the Bible passage.

If you believe you have to feel *happy* about all of the things that happen in your life, you are doomed to frustration, anger, and a whole lot of stress. Even Jesus wasn't delighted with everything that occurred in his life. When his disciples woke him up during the storm in Matthew 8, he didn't say, "Thank you for interrupting my nap." In fact, he seemed to be more than a little irritated, saying, "Why are you afraid, O men of little faith?" His mood doesn't appear to have instantly improved after the storm subsided, because the apostles seemed afraid to talk directly to him. They said to themselves, "What sort of man is this, that even winds and sea obey him?" It's obvious that if Jesus didn't have warm, fuzzy feelings all the time, we can't expect them either.

Which brings us to the Bible verse that we so often misread. It doesn't say, "Give thanks *for* all circumstances." It says, "Give thanks *in* all circumstances." The distinction is that we don't have to have feelings of happiness or pleasure *about* a situation in order to give thanks *in* the situation.

> *Gratefulness is the key to a happy life that we hold in our hands, because if we are not grateful, then no matter how much we have we will not be happy — because we will always want to have something else or something more.*
> — BR. DAVID STEINDL-RAST

Maybe an example from my life will help clarify what I mean.

I live in a two-story house, with the guest bath directly above my home office. One winter's night I heard an odd crashing noise. But, because I had a very adventuresome Abyssinian cat at the time, crashing noises were common. I figured he had knocked over a bookcase and broken a vase. A few minutes later, however, I noticed water dripping down the walls of my office. Racing upstairs, I waded into a flooded bathroom to discover a shattered toilet. The entire toilet had broken into pieces, pulling the water line from the wall. I tried to shut off the water, but the valve was broken, and all I could do was slow the gushing. Racing out into the dark, I managed to find the main shutoff for the water line. A friend with plumbing experience came over to help me seal off the interior pipe and turn the main line back on. I then mopped up the floor and picked up the pieces of broken porcelain. By the time I was done, it was well past midnight. If you think at that moment that I fell to my knees telling God how really grateful I was that I had a flooded bathroom and a broken water pipe, you're nuts.

It was at about this time, however, that I had begun to try to find God's grace in all the events of my life. Once the immediate cleanup was finished, I sat down at my desk and looked around my office. Despite the fact that the room contained all sorts of electronic equipment — two computers, a printer, a fax, and an answering machine — as well as stacks of papers and books, the only thing that had been damaged from the water was the surge protector. Apparently it had turned off the equipment and then shorted out. Everything else was just fine.

Now, I *did* give thanks. Not for the plumbing disaster but because even in the disaster, God had been with me. I was grateful — not for what had happened, but for what had not happened.

Gratitude and the Simple Life

So how does this relate to simplifying life — which is, after all, the reason you're reading this book?

Once my attention was centered in gratitude, my stress level immediately shifted. I moved into a state where I could think more clearly. All I really had to do was clean up some water and call a plumber. I might not like it, but I could handle it. It was no longer nearly as big of a deal as it had been. All because I had found something to be thankful for *in* the situation. Not *for* the situation, but in it.

As time has gone on, I've gotten better at making this kind of shift in all kinds of circumstances. Time and again I've discovered that when I move mentally to looking for what's right instead of what's wrong, I am less stressed; solutions present themselves more quickly; I am able to deal with life's inevitable problems more rationally; and life is just plain simpler.

In, *Not* For

It's not a matter of being a Pollyanna, pretending that bad things haven't happened. Rather, it's a case of looking for the abundance and blessing that is present in every situation, no matter how dire it may appear. A friend of mine, who is one of my mentors in learning this secret, recently gave me a beautiful example.

About six months ago, she had a melanoma removed, and the doctors gave her a clean bill of health. Then, a few weeks ago, she noticed a lump. After a series of tests, she was told the melanoma had returned and metastasized. With her permission, I'm sharing the e-mail she sent after she received the news.

> I definitely have melanoma. They cannot give me the two drugs that are most effective to calm it and back it off. Those would require hospitalization for a week to administer them, and they can cause devastating heart attacks. My doctor believes I would not survive....

When you are grateful, fear disappears and abundance appears.

— ANTHONY ROBBINS

Although she is realistic about her situation, she immediately shifts to a place of gratitude:

> The surgeon told me I am in spectacular health, so should tolerate treatments well. One of the things they do now is vaccines. Also interferon. A lot of research is being done at Providence Cancer Center, so I will have access to the latest and best, whatever it is. I might even be in a study.... I am unbelievably calm about this. (It's a God thing, I'm sure, from all the prayers going up.) Because I am not panicky, Dick (her husband) goes along with my hopefulness, far as I can tell. It is now suppertime, so must go cook. We are having baked Alaska salmon, rice, pickled asparagus, and other veggies of some kind. Will sit by the fireplace tonight and read Sarah Palin's book. Oh, and also the Susan Boyle CD is just beautiful. What a voice!

Even in the midst of sharing a horrendous diagnosis, my friend expresses gratitude for her overall health, the medical care available, the simple pleasure of a delicious dinner, a book to read, and the beauty of music.

Looking in All the Right Places

Which brings me to another important aspect of gratitude: You have to look for something to be thankful for every day. It isn't easy. It doesn't come naturally to most of us. We have to deliberately, consciously keep our eyes open. But here's something that never fails to amaze me — the more you look for things to be grateful for, the more things you will find to be grateful for.

A friend and I decided about a year ago to look for what we call the "abundance" in our lives, based on Jesus' promise that he came so that we "may have life, and have it abundantly." Anything over and above what we expected to receive that day we called "abundance." It might be as small as finding a dime on the sidewalk or as major as having the interest rate reduced on the mortgage, but if it wasn't something we had been anticipating, if it came to us unexpectedly as gift, it was abundance.

At first, we had to go over our days carefully to find abundance. Eventually, we went from searching for abundance to excitedly watching for it. It was quite fun to wait and see what blessing we would be given.

Feeling gratitude and not expressing it is like wrapping a present and not giving it.

— WILLIAM ARTHUR WARD

Then, for whatever reason, we began to grow complacent. We no longer shared our abundance on a regular basis. We no longer gave daily thanks. One day, as we were talking, she asked me what abundance I had received that day. I had to stop and think. I couldn't recall anything special. "I don't think I had an abundance today," I sheepishly admitted.

"Me, neither," she said. "I think it's because we stopped looking for it."

We'd both had the same experience. When we were looking for blessings, for things to be grateful for, our lives were overflowing with them. We truly experienced abundance. As soon as we stopped looking for it and being grateful for it, however, the abundance evaporated. It's not that God had stopped offering us his gifts. It was like we had dammed the river of blessing by our failure to acknowledge it in gratitude. As soon as we began our daily practice, we once again experienced an overflow of things to be thankful about.

> *Both abundance and lack exist simultaneously in our lives, as parallel realities. It is always our conscious choice which secret garden we will tend. . . . When we choose not to focus on what is missing from our lives but are grateful for the abundance that's present — love, health, family, friends, work, the joys of nature and personal pursuits that bring us pleasure — the wasteland of illusion falls away, and we experience Heaven on earth.*
>
> — SARAH BAN BREATHNACH

What does all of this have to do with simplification? Living more simply allows me the time to recognize blessings received; then, ironically, the blessings and abundance I receive seem to make my life simpler and easier. I find change in the pocket of a jacket I haven't worn for months, just when I need to feed a meter. The gas tank stays full enough for me to run all my errands and get to the gas station without stress. An editor calls and tells me that I have an extra week on a deadline because she is going to be out of town. The very act of living in a state of gratitude makes the whole of my life simpler.

Applied daily, it will do the same for you. In fact, it will make all of your life

Simply Abundant!

Take Away

If the only prayer you said in your whole life was, "Thank you," that would suffice.

— MEISTER ECKHART

A Prayer for Simplicity

Dear God,
Help me to notice the falling of the snowflake
The flight of the birds
The light in a child's eye
Help me to understand that my life is not made more
  meaningful by what I have,
Nor less by what I do not have.
Help me to see the abundance in my life and to know
  that I am enough.
Lead me to the quiet reverence that comes from the
  abiding spirit of simplicity
As one human being who walks this earth
Among countless others who have walked before me
And who will follow me when I am gone.
Lead me to the simple joy of acceptance,
of myself, of my life and your Divine Plan.
Amen.

— ROBERT H. COLEMAN